BURNIN' RUBBER

BURNIN' RUBBER

Behind the Scenes in Stock Car Racing

GEORGE SULLIVAN

THE MILLBROOK PRESS

Brookfield, Connecticut

Library of Congress Cataloging-in-Publication Data
Sullivan, George, 1927–
Burnin' rubber : behind the scenes in stock car racing / George Sullivan.
p.   cm.
Includes index.
Summary: describes how stock cars are created, the work of the race
team and pit crew, experiences on the racing circuit, and more.
ISBN 0-7613-1256-0
1. Stock car racing—Juvenile literature. 2. Automobiles, Racing—
Juvenile literature. 3. Automobile racing drivers—Juvenile literature.
[1. Stock car racing.] I. Title.
GV1029.9.S74S85   1998
796.72'0973—DC21   97-27102   CIP   AC

Published by The Millbrook Press, Inc.
2 Old New Milford Road
Brookfield, Connecticut 06804

Photo credits

Charlotte Motor Speedway, courtesy of Christine Pinto, p. 2;
Darlington Raceway, p. 13; Featherlite Trailers, pp. 16, 19; Hendrick
Motorsports, p. 27; IMS Properties, Steve Ellis, p. 35, and Walt
Kuhn, p. 37; Michigan International Speedway, Jim Cutler, courtesy
of Tommy Cameron, p. 29; Performance PR Plus, p. 20; Phoenix
International Raceway, Leroy Clark, p. 11; George Sullivan, pp. 17,
18, 23, 28, 30, 34, 40; Talladega Superspeedway, pp. 24, 33, 41;
Wide World, pp. 10, 22, 31, 39, 43.

Acknowledgments

The author is grateful to the many racing specialists and experts who provided information and advice during the time this book was being written, some of whom read sections of the manuscript for accuracy. Special thanks are due Andy Hall, Director of Public Relations, and Tracy Eberts and Maria Harley, NASCAR; Kevin Davey and Pat Jones, IMS Licensing; Al Robinson, Dover Downs International Speedway; Russell Branham, Darlington Raceway; Kirk Turnmire and Matt Baumann, Featherlite Trailers; Michelle Norman, Sears Point Raceway; Scott Simpson, Phoenix International Raceway; Kenneth Campbell, Richmond International Raceway; Ron Miller, Performance PR Plus; Bill Broderick, 76 Products Company; Patti Angeloni, Pocono Raceway; Danielle Humphrey, DMF Communications; Tommy Cameron, Michigan International Speedway; Lorraine Faford, New Hampshire International Speedway; Richard Sowers, Atlanta Motor Speedway; Dick Thompson, Martinsville Speedway; Linda DeBlois and Pat Sanborn, QVC; John Ervin, Robert Yates Racing; Troy Brady, Barbasol Racing; Steve Covell, MBNA; Charles Brandt, Wilmington Delaware; Christine Pinto, Charlotte Motor Speedway; and Bill Thompson.

Contents

1

Fast Sport, Fast Growth

Imagine 40 or so brightly painted two-door passenger cars screaming around a race track at awe-
some speeds. They hurry through the turns and go
"bumpin' 'n' jammin'" into the straights. More than
100,000 fans watch in delight.

Early in the race, a car heads into the wall, its tires
skidding and screeching—"burnin' rubber." Suddenly it bursts into flames and black smoke gushes
from the engine. The crowd looks on in a mixture
of horror and fascination.

As a red van speeds onto the track and toward the
burning car, a yellow caution flag warns drivers to
slow down and hold their positions. Men in fire-
resistant suits spray a white, pastelike chemical over
the vehicle. The driver is helped from the car and
into an ambulance.

Once the car is hauled from the track, the race
resumes. At the famed Daytona International Speedway, cars flash around the 2 1/2–mile layout in 45
seconds. You have to be able to pilot a car at 200
miles an hour to qualify at Daytona. At that speed,
you could cover a football field from end zone to
end zone in just one second.

The race at Daytona, a D-shaped course, is known
as the Daytona 500 because it covers 500 miles. A
grinding test that lasts more than three hours, it

Part of a nine-car pileup that took place just two laps from the finish line during the Goody's Headache Powder 300 race at Daytona International Speedway in 1995.

exhausts drivers. But the rewards can be worth the struggle. The prize fund at Daytona is slightly more than $4 million.

Colorful cars traveling at breakneck speeds. Gritty and determined drivers. Frenzied fans. Big money prizes. That's stock car racing. For sheer drama and excitement—and danger—no other sport can match it.

The cars that race in the Winston Cup series, the name given to the series of races in which the fastest, most powerful stock cars compete, look like late models of ordinary Fords, Chevrolets, or Pontiacs, the kind you might see in a supermarket parking lot. That's a big part of the sport's attraction.

But the car's chassis— that is, the frame and the wheels on which the body is supported, and the body itself — has been altered. And the engine has been rebuilt to produce the fastest speeds possible.

Stock cars race mostly on oval tracks that range in size from $1/2$ mile to 2 $1/2$ miles. Those tracks that cover a mile or more are known as super-speedways. On superspeedways, with their long straights and wide, high–banked turns, cars travel the fastest.

The Talladega (Alabama) Superspeedway is the fastest track of all. Bill Elliott, in qualifying, set a record there in 1987 with an average speed of 212.8 miles per hour. The record still stands.

At Watkins Glen, New York, and Sonoma, California, stock cars compete on exciting road courses that feature gentle hills and sharp turns. Sears Point Raceway, at Sonoma, is a stern test of a driver's ability to get around corners. There are twelve turns at Sears Point.

About half of the races in the Winston Cup series are 500 miles, and most of the others are almost that long. The Charlotte (North Carolina) Motor Speedway offers the longest race—600 miles.

Once limited to the Southeast, where stock car racing began, the sport is now as national as baseball or Burger King. The Winston Cup series includes

Stock cars look like late models of standard Fords, Chevrolets, or Pontiacs, but have much more power and speed. Here, Terry Labonte, twice Winston Cup champion, competes in his Chevy Monte Carlo at the Phoenix International Raceway.

slightly more than 30 races at some 20 different tracks. (Some tracks offer two Winston Cup races each season.)

There are stops at the Indianapolis Motor Speedway, the New Hampshire International Speedway, the Texas Motor Speedway in Roanoke, just north of Fort Worth, and the California Speedway in Fontana, east of Los Angeles.

These, of course, are in addition to the sport's traditional races in Daytona Beach, Florida; Darlington, South Carolina; and Talladega, Alabama.

Besides its coast-to-coast appeal, there are plenty of other ways to measure the booming popularity of stock car racing. Attendance at Winston Cup races has doubled and redoubled in recent years. Television ratings are the highest in history.

What's unusual about stock car racing's tremendous popularity is that it happened so fast. Stock car racing had its beginnings in the piney woods and rugged mountains of the Southeast during the mid-1930s. There, the making and selling of homemade whiskey was often used as a source of family income. Since the whiskey was illegal, "runner cars" delivering the liquor had to be superfast, able to outrun the sheriff or federal tax officials. Sometimes the "boys" who drove the runner cars would test their talents in local races held on back roads or dirt tracks laid out in cow pastures. As the races became more and more popular, people began paying to watch.

Growth of the sport was hindered by a lack of organization. Rules varied from track to track, which made it difficult for drivers to compete at every course. The sport took a giant step forward in 1947 when Bill France, a mechanic, driver, and race promoter, held a meeting at the Streamline Hotel in Daytona Beach with about 35 other stock car drivers and race promoters. Out of that meeting came NASCAR, the National Association of Stock Car Auto Racing, a name suggested by Jerome "Red" Vogt, a well-known driver from Atlanta.

Bill France was elected NASCAR's first president. Erwin "Cannonball" Baker was named the organization's first commissioner. Then in his seventies, Baker was known around the world for his racing heroics, mostly in endurance competition.

NASCAR put all of stock car racing under one set of rules. It also established a point system for determining a national driving champion each year.

In the years that followed the birth of NASCAR, stock car building and racing zoomed in popularity throughout the Southeast. The construction of the Daytona International Speedway, with its steep turns,

Darlington Raceway is called "the grandaddy of the superspeedways." Its unique shape, with one end of the oval wider than the other, has helped to make Darlington one of the toughest courses on the NASCAR circuit.

helped to trigger interest and support in stock car racing from General Motors, Ford, and Chrysler.

Lee Petty won the first Daytona 500 in an Olds. Petty's average speed of 135.5 miles an hour shocked racing fans of the time. No one had come close to that speed before. Modern superspeedways were planned in Darlington (South Carolina), Atlanta, Charlotte, and other locations.

Stock car racing began going big time in 1971 when NASCAR teamed up with Winston cigarettes and introduced the Winston Cup competitions. Before the decade ended, the television networks were providing live coverage of races.

In recent years, the sport's popularity can be judged by what's happened to NASCAR. NASCAR has become a brand name. You can order a burger at a NASCAR Cafe, load up on clothing and souvenirs at a NASCAR Thunder retail store, or zip around the high–banked turns of a NASCAR Speed Park in a frisky cart, a miniature automobile designed especially for racing.

If you're already a fan of stock car racing, or are thinking of becoming one, you can get up-to-the-minute information on any one of NASCAR's twelve racing divisions, including the Winston Cup series, from NASCAR's official Internet site. It's on the World Wide Web at: http://www.nascar.com.

Bill France, "Red" Vogt, "Cannonball" Baker, and other of the sport's pioneers could never have imagined what stock car racing has become.

2

The Car

NASCAR stock cars are not really race cars—at first. Car owners take basic body shapes of two-door American passenger cars, fit them out with powerful engines, and convert them into racing machines.

In recent years, only three different cars have been raced in Winston Cup competition. They are the Ford Thunderbird, Chevrolet Monte Carlo, and Pontiac Grand Prix.

In creating a stock car, the race team begins with the chassis, the frame and wheels on which the body is supported. The engine comes next. Each engine is custom-built.

The engine for Dale Earnhardt's black Chevrolet, sponsored by Goodwrench, is built at Richard Childress Racing in Welcome, North Carolina. It is able to generate more than 700 horsepower. (The engine for the average family automobile is rated at about 160 horsepower.) The powerful RCR engines have helped to make Earnhardt a dominant force in Winston Cup racing.

Earnhardt, like other drivers, requires not merely one engine, but a number of them. One engine is needed for practice, another for qualifying, and two race engines, one a backup, are required.

Once an engine has completed a race, it's retired.

It goes back to the RCR shop where it is completely rebuilt. The block, the heavy casting into which the cylinders and other parts fit, is reused, but most parts are brand-new. Earnhardt's budget for engines and engine work is around $1 million a year.

Tires are another big expense. The typical Winston Cup car chews up 360 sets—a total of 1,440 tires—each racing season. At $300 apiece, that's $432,000 for tires.

Not all tires in a set of four are the same size. The outside tires are a little bit bigger than those on the inside. This is because the outside tires, when going around a turn, have to travel a greater distance than those on the inside. They are made bigger to make up for the increased wear to which they're exposed.

In a typical set of four tires, the two inside tires are 86 inches in circumference. The distance around the two outside tires is at least 87 inches. And the front outside tire, which gets more wear than any other, is a fraction of an inch bigger in circumfer-

The typical stock car engine generates about 700 horsepower. This one powers Bobby Hamilton's STP Pontiac.

Some of the special racing tires delivered to Dover Downs International Speedway for the running of the MBNA 500.

ence than the back outside tire. In other words, the front outside tire is the biggest tire of all.

Tire pressure is also different from tire to tire. The right front tire has the most pressure; the left front, the least. Tire pressure varies from track to track, too, depending on the track surface and other conditions.

All race car tires are also equipped with a plastic safety liner, an inner surface that acts to support the car should the outer tire wear down. Should a tire fail, the safety shield acts like a tire within the tire, which enables the car to keep moving.

Creating a stock car is not just a matter of getting a chassis, an engine, and all the parts and putting them together. The overall shape of the car is a critical matter. The race team wants its car to slice through the air like a low-flying missile.

This means that the team has to be concerned with such matters as downforce, which is heavy downward pressure created by airflow and drag. The more downforce a car has, the better it sticks to the track. In a car with a lot of downforce, the driver doesn't have to worry that he might suddenly veer into a wall or another car. He can hold the car wide open more.

Stock cars rely on an air deflector called a *spoiler* to help create downforce. A narrow metal panel 57 inches in length, the spoiler is mounted atop the car's rear deck.

Raising the spoiler increases the car's grip. Low-ering the spoiler reduces it. But a race team is not permitted to raise or lower the spoiler at will. The team follows the spoiler standards issued by NASCAR for all cars.

Drag—anything that tends to retard the forward motion of the car—is another important factor. Race teams, naturally, try to reduce drag as much as possible. For example, stock car headlights are replaced with flat pieces of aluminum to reduce drag. In a 500-mile race, this can mean miles of difference.

To get the shape of the car as sleek as possible, race

Air-deflecting panel mounted atop car's rear deck is called a spoiler.

Huge transporters haul race cars and equipment from one track to the next. This one belongs to Dale Earnhardt's Goodwrench team.

teams do wind tunnel testing. A stream of air is blown at the car body, which helps to reveal the effects of wind, or airflow, on it. "Without tunnel testing," says one crew member, "you can't be competitive."

Besides the car bodies and engines, thousands of dollars in spare parts are required. Tools and equipment are another big expense.

Each team also needs a hauler, an enormous semi–trailer to transport its cars and its equipment from one race site to another. A hauler and its truck tractor can cost as much as half a million dollars.

And there are salaries to be paid. There is the driver's salary, another half million dollars or so. There are salaries for the crew chief, the shop crew, the pit crew, and office staff. There are travel expenses and lodging and meals for the driver and the crew.

All of this adds up to several million dollars for a season of racing. But no car owner has become a charity case. At the same time the owner is spending money like water, he is taking in money from sponsors. Corporations pay huge amounts to display their names, symbols, or trademarks on car bodies.

Most stock car teams have a primary sponsor that pays $3 million to $4 million dollars a year to advertise on the car's hood and sides. Another sponsor is likely to pay as much as $1 million to put its name on the edge of the trunk lid. This is called the TV panel because it can be seen from the in-car television cameras in other drivers' cars during race telecasts. This makes it especially valuable. A couple of dozen small decals adorn each side of the car forward of the doors. The space each of these decals occupies sells for from $500 to $2,000.

In addition to selling space on the car's body, the car's owner looks forward to winning prize money. This can be a sizeable amount. In 1995, for instance, in 31 races, Jeff Gordon won $4,347,343 in prize money. Ordinarily, the driver and the sponsor divide the prize money equally, meaning that Gordon's sponsor, DuPont Automotive finishes, received $2,173,671 in winnings.

The trick, of course, is to get enough income to cover one's expenses and perhaps even earn a profit. That's the challenge every stock car owner faces.

Sponsors pay millions of dollars to advertise on race cars—and on driver's uniforms, too. Here, Jeff Gordon, Winston Cup champion in 1995 and winner of ten races in 1996, poses with his colorful Chevy Monte Carlo.

3

Behind the Wheel

Suppose you were asked to take a NASCAR stock car on a practice run. What would it be like?

Before you enter the car, you would have to put on the fire–resistant clothing that all drivers wear. It includes a three–layer Nomex suit and Nomex head sock. Drivers even wear fireproof underwear.

Your first surprise may be to find that the two car doors are welded shut. This helps make the car safer. In case of a head–on crash, the doors collapse, absorbing some of the impact.

Since the doors don't open, you have to enter the car through the driver's side window. You first reach in and remove the steering wheel so you'll have room to maneuver. It lifts off easily. Grasping the roof above the door, you slip into the car feet first and drop into the deeply contoured, heavily braced, wraparound seat.

You hitch up the five-point, double-width Simpson harness that holds you tightly to the seat, then put on your full-face, hard-shell Bell helmet. Now you look like a driver. You feel like one, too.

When you attach the steering wheel to the steering column, the wheel is only inches from your face. Your hands are close to your chest when you grasp it. Positioning the wheel like this helps to relieve driver fatigue during the hours it takes to complete a

Bill Elliott prepares to climb into his Ford Thunderbird before a race at the Talladega Superspeedway.

400-or 500-mile race, it's been found. But it takes some time to get used to the setup.

A member of your crew lifts the fabric net covering the window on the driver's side and snaps it in place. (There is no pane of glass or clear plastic in the window on the driver's side.) The other windows are sheet plastic and sealed shut.

The window net is meant to keep the driver's head and left arm from plunging through the window opening in the event of a crash. It unsnaps easily in case emergency crews have to get to the driver fast.

Across the inside of the roof and behind your head are heavy steel roll bars. These brace the frame of the car and are meant to prevent the roof from collapsing should the car flip over.

On the floor beneath your feet there's a heavy thermal insulating pad. This prevents the intense heat from the engine from frying the soles of your shoes. The engine's exhaust pipe, which runs under the floor, heats up the cockpit even more.

As the car speeds along, a pair of scoops on the passenger side of the car in front of and just behind the front window draws air into thick plastic tubes. This air cools the car's lubricants. In case of a crash and fire, there's a fire extinguisher just to your right. To make it spray, all you have to do is pull a cable and hit the extinguisher's plunger.

The dashboard is very simple when compared to the dash of a family automobile. Four small dials report water temperature, oil temperature, oil pressure, and amount of fuel. A red warning light flashes when oil pressure gets too low.

There's no speedometer. Instead, you check a large circular dial called a tachometer. This reports engine revolutions per minute, or rpm's. From these, the driver can estimate his speed. When leaving or entering the pit road, he knows that speed must be sharply reduced, perhaps to 50 miles per hour, and the rpm's must be below 3,000.

During each lap, a car's speed varies, depending on which part of the track it happens to be covering. It travels fastest on straights, slowest on turns. So drivers aren't concerned about their speed as reported in miles per hour at any given moment. Their lap time is what's important—how long it takes to make a complete circuit of the track.

A two-way radio that links the driver with his crew is mounted on the door on the driver's side. As the driver circles the track, the crew chief calls out lap times in seconds. For example, at Daytona International Speedway, a 2 1/2-mile layout, the crew chief might report a lap time of 52.6 (which is the equivalent of 171 miles per hour).

To start the car, you flip a small switch on the

Dashboards are kept simple. Large dial is a tachometer.

left–hand side of the dashboard and step on the gas. The 700-horsepower engine roars to life. (It's this switch the driver flips when he hears the track announcer call out, "Drivers, start your engines!") There's no ignition key involved.

Most of today's stock cars are equipped with a 4-speed transmission system, but it's usually not automatic, not clutchless. There's a shifter mounted close to your right hand. You press on the clutch and pull the handle to shift gears.

As you come out of the pit and onto the track, you're likely to be impressed at how smoothly the car handles. Despite its weight, 3,500 pounds, it steers easily as you cruise through the first two turns and

into the back straight. Be sure to keep both hands on the wheel, the left hand at 9 o'clock, the right hand at 3 o'clock. This positioning enables you to make lane changes without shifting hands.

During your practice run, it's smart to keep within the groove, the continuous strip of black, about 12 feet wide, that's been laid down on the track surface by car tires. Not only is it the quickest way around the track, it's the safest. On the straights, the band of black clings to the outside, close to the wall. As you come into a turn, it dives for the inside, close to the infield. Veer outside of the groove and you could be asking for trouble.

When you brake to slow down, notice how quickly the four-wheel disc brakes respond. Get into the habit of braking before you start turning. Braking thrusts the weight of the car to the front, but if you brake before the turn, then release the brakes, the weight distribution evens out. All four tires help in getting you around the turn.

When your run is over and you head back to the pit, downshift and touch the brake pedal to slow down and stop. Once you're back at your starting point, the crew chief hands you a cool drink through the window after the netting is unsnapped. When you decide to exit, don't look for a door handle. Remember, you have to crawl back out through the window.

Drivers keep to the outside on straights, then dive to the inside on turns.

4

The Team

Young Jeff Gordon is one of the most successful drivers of recent years, if not *the* most successful. Gordon won seven races in 1995, and ten in 1996. He took home an all-time record $4,347,343 in prize money in 1995.

He began 1997 by winning the Daytona 500, becoming, at twenty–five, the youngest winner in the race's history. The next week, Jeff won at the North Carolina Motor Speedway. After each of his victories, Gordon never failed to credit Rick Hendrick and Ray Evernham. Hendrick owns and builds the cars that Gordon races. Evernham, as Jeff Gordon's crew chief, heads the group of highly trained specialists who are responsible for the way his cars perform. Like other drivers, Jeff realizes that success in stock car racing comes from teamwork. Winning is a joint effort on the part of the driver, the crew chief, and the owner.

Each of Gordon's cars is built from the ground up at Hendrick's shops in Harrisburg, North Carolina, about two miles from the Charlotte Motor Speedway. Hendrick also builds cars for Terry Labonte, the Winston Cup champion in 1996. The Hendrick complex includes completely equipped shops—an engine shop, chassis shop, cylinder-head shop, paint shop. There's also a gym for drivers and crew members, and a museum. The operation employs 150 people. Visitors are welcome.

Hendrick's shops are designed so that a racing team can drive its massive hauler in one side for loading or unloading. It can then drive out the other side without having to back up or turn around. Hendrick owns car dealerships up and down the East Coast. According to *The Wall Street Journal*, he is America's biggest car dealer. For his racing empire, Hendrick hires the best people, pays them well, and inspires them to work hard. Everyone has the same goal: to get the cars to go faster.

When Jeff Gordon was about to be hired by Hendrick, he was asked who he preferred as a crew chief. Jeff said, "Ray." Ray Evernham, a former driver, had been Jeff's crew chief at an earlier stage of his career. The two are best friends.

In days past, the stock car crew was made up of a driver and his mechanic. They did everything. It's much different today. The shop crew, like a football team, is made up of specialists. They include a chassis specialist, a motor expert, and a body man. Some shop crew members travel with the car and help prepare it for the race. Others remain at the shops. At the track, the hauler that transports the car serves as the crew's headquarters.

Not long after the car arrives at the track, the driver takes it through a few practice laps. Afterward, he discusses the car's performance with the crew chief, who then instructs his crew to make whatever adjustments are needed to improve the way the car handles. In track lingo, they "set up" the car for the race.

Rick Hendrick built and owned cars raced by such superstar drivers as Jeff Gordon and Terry Labonte.

Critical adjustments are made to the car's shock absorbers and its suspension system. These adjustments differ from track to track, depending on the size of the race course, the tightness of the turns, and the amount of banking on the turns. A car that is to race at the Daytona International Speedway, with its high-banked turns which tilt a car almost onto its side, has to be set up much differently than a car that is to compete at the Indianapolis Motor Speedway, which has long straights.

Throughout the race day, crew members must haul tires from the garage area to pits.

A car's tires get a lot of attention. Several sets of tires are needed for each race. Each tire is mounted on a rim and brought to the pit area to await use.

Some tracks require more tires than others. Dover (Delaware) Downs International Speedway, as the only concrete track on the Winston Cup circuit, chews up tires at a faster rate than any of the black–topped tracks. A car may require as many as 10 or 11 sets of tires during a 500-mile race at Dover.

Sometimes major repairs are required in the hours before a race. Before a 500–mile race at the Pocono Speedway in 1996, Rusty Wallace's crew discovered a cracked engine block in his Ford Thunderbird. The crew had only about two hours to install a new engine. Four crew members were involved.

First, the damaged engine had to come out. Crew members unscrewed the engine bolts and disconnected the various hoses, then drained the engine of all its fluids—oil, water, and coolants. The engine was then connected to a hoist and lifted out of the engine bay.

Meanwhile, the new engine was taken from the transporter, brought to the garage area, attached to the hoist, and lowered into the car. Hoses were connected and nuts tightened. Engine fluids were replaced.

Fresh tires, fuel, and a clean windshield for Kyle Petty's Pontiac Grand Prix during pit stop at Michigan International Speedway.

Once the engine was in place, it had to be checked by NASCAR officials to make certain that it met official standards. The engine change went off without a hitch. Wallace took his place at the start as if nothing had happened.

Fans are usually unaware of all the tuning and maintenance work that goes on in the garage area. It's during pit stops that fans become alert to a crew's value. The pit itself is the area just off the track with space for each car to be refueled, have its tires changed, and repairs made. In stock car racing, the pits are located on a roadway that runs parallel to the main straightaway.

Some members of the pit crew are drawn from the shop crew. Others are hired for a particular race. NASCAR rules permit only six team members to go over the wall to service a car during a pit stop. The men pounce on the car the instant it comes to a stop, then work frantically.

While one cleans the windshield, two gasmen fuel the car. Each, in turn, pours gas from an 11-gallon,

To speed tire changes, lug nuts are glued in place before the race.

cylinder-shaped canister into the car's 22-gallon tank. Once the jackman has jacked up one side of the car, two other crew members change the tires on that side. A skilled crew is capable of changing the two outside tires (those that get the most wear), refueling the car, cleaning the windshield, and providing the driver with a cooling drink in 12 or 13 seconds.

A tire change can be completed in the blink of an eye. The instant the car is raised by a jack, one team member removes the five lug nuts holding the tire in place. He uses a compressed-air wrench to speed the operation. As he removes the tire, another crew member puts the new tire in place. No one has to fiddle with the lug nuts. They've already been glued in place on the rim. It's then a simple matter of matching the holes and lug nuts with the threaded rods onto which they fit. Once the rim is in place, it takes only a split second to tighten the lug nuts with the air wrench.

Every second is vital. At the Daytona International Speedway, one second spent in the pit is equal to 300 feet on the track. A fast crew makes the difference as to whether a car finishes in the top five or back in the pack.

Since NASCAR rules permit only a very limited amount of fuel to be stored in the pit, crew members must constantly haul more fuel from the garage

After driver Robby Gordon crashed during race at Talladega Superspeedway, his pit crew was presented with more than the usual set of problems.

area. Fresh tires must be brought from the garage, too. "The best race isn't the one on the track," says one crew member. "It's the race between pit crews back and forth to the garage as they try to keep their cars supplied with fuel and tires. They're always on the run."

During breaks, pit crews follow the race action by means of a television monitor. A special NASCAR closed-circuit broadcast gives the race standings every two laps.

When the race is over, the winning driver never fails to hail the victory as a team effort.

"When this car wins, we *all* win," each driver says. "When it loses, we *all* lose."

5

Race Day

To stock car fans, it's a scene that starts their hearts pounding. It's one that's repeated 30 or so times a year.

The long colorful string of cars in double file follows the pace car around the track. Faster and faster they go. As the line of cars approaches the starting line, the green flag falls.

The huge crowd stands and cheers. The cars, each jockeying for a better position, surge into Turn One.

Almost always, that scene takes place early on a Sunday afternoon. The day's activities, however, begin long before the race's start. On race day, the track opens as early as 5 o'clock in the morning to admit the first fans. They drive pickups or RVs and purchase tickets which admit them and their vehicles to the infield area. Some fans prepare breakfast on portable stoves. Others sunbathe or snooze atop their vehicles.

The grandstand opens at 8 o'clock and more fans pour in. Many wear shirts or caps that feature the name or car number of their favorite driver. Dale Earnhardt, one of the most popular drivers, drives

Fans jam the infield to await the start of race action at the Talladega Superspeedway.

a black Monte Carlo Chevy blazoned with the number 3. At any given race, thousands of fans wear black T-shirts bearing the number 3 or black caps with Earnhardt's autograph.

Stands that have been erected just outside the

Driver Randy LaJoie autographs a fan's prize T-shirt before a race at Dover Downs International Speedway.

track offer a great array of clothing and souvenirs. A fan can buy shirts, belts, shoelaces, and even underwear with the name and number of his or her favorite driver.

Earplugs are essential for race fans. Even in the early morning hours, with only a few cars running practice runs, the constant high-pitched clatter of powerful engines is tough on the eardrums. Foam rubber earplugs offer needed protection.

Some fans prefer to cover their ears with headphones that are linked to scanners. These permit the wearer to listen to communications between a driver and his crew chief and learn race strategy. There might be a discussion of the car's fuel situation or how many tires to change at the next pit stop. Scanners have much the same technology as the "scan" option on a car radio. They search the radio frequencies until they find activity.

Fan scanners, however, are usually set up to monitor the frequency of a particular driver. Drivers realize that scanners offer their rival teams the opportunity to listen in on their conversations with their crew chiefs. As a result, drivers are cautious about what they say on their radios, and sometimes teams abruptly change frequencies without telling outsiders.

Double file of cars enters Turn Two at the Indianapolis Motor Speedway during pace lap for the Brickyard 400.

As the early fans are getting settled, the garage area is bursting with activity as cars are checked and rechecked and last-minute adjustments are made.

Not every car and driver that shows up gets to race. In the days before the event, qualifying rounds are held to determine which drivers will compete and which ones will go home early. The qualifying rounds are also used to determine each driver's position at the start of the race. The faster one's qualifying time, the better one's position.

The best starting position is the pole position. At the race's start, cars line up two-by-two in about 20 rows. The pole position is in the first row closest to the infield. Since this position offers the shortest distance around the track, it is the starting position that every driver wants.

Drivers attempt to qualify one at a time, seeking to achieve the best possible lap time. No other cars are on the track. Competition is fierce because everyone wants a good starting position.

Watching a car speed around a track all by itself may not seem very exciting to watch, yet thousands of fans turn out. Some bring stopwatches to time their favorite drivers, comparing their readings to the track announcer's reports.

Occasionally there is a tense moment. At Daytona one year, Bill Elliott was speeding around the oval with no one else on the track when his engine began to leak oil. Once all the oil had drained out, the engine suddenly quit. Elliott struggled to keep control but he could not. He smacked into the wall, wrecking the car.

Before a car can compete in a race, it has to be inspected by NASCAR officials to be sure it complies with the organization's rules and regulations. Cars are inspected in the days before a race. The crew elevates the car on four jack stands. Inspectors check different engine parts, such as the carburetor, the device that mixes air into the fuel. They measure how much fuel the fuel tank can hold. Each car is permitted only 22 gallons of fuel. Each car is also weighed. NASCAR rules state that a car cannot weigh more than 3,500 pounds.

At about 10 o'clock on the day of the race, drivers and their crew chiefs attend a meeting to discuss the race and resolve any questions that they might have. Following the meeting, there is a chapel service for drivers and crew chiefs.

Pre-race activities for the fans begin at 11 o'clock. Drivers follow the pace car on a parade lap around the track. Afterward, with the cars lined up two abreast on the track, the drivers are introduced one-by-one.

Not long after noon, the drivers prepare for the race start. They climb into their cars, fasten their seat harnesses, and put on their helmets. "Drivers, start your engines!" says the starter. The cars, still parked two by two, roar to life. An afternoon of thrills and excitement is about to begin.

Green flag drops to signal the start of the Brickyard 400. At right, pace car has pulled off the track.

6

How to Win

They call it Dale Earnhardt's "pass in the grass." It took place at the Charlotte Motor Speedway several years ago. It is one of the most famous winning moves in stock car history.

There were seven laps to go in what had been one of the roughest races in years. Earnhardt and Bill Elliott were involved in a fierce fender-bending struggle almost from the start.

As the two cars came out of Turn Four and went rocketing into the straight in front of the stands, Earnhardt was leading. Then Elliott nudged Earnhardt with his bumper from behind. Earnhardt's car veered off the race course and onto a grassy stretch adjacent to the track.

Earnhardt never took his foot off the gas. His car shivered and shook, but Earnhardt stayed with it. And when the car charged back onto the track, Earnhardt was still in the lead. And he went on to win the race.

At Martinsville (Virginia) Speedway in 1994, Kenny Wallace bumped Earnhardt, and Earnhardt did a 360-degree spin. But Earnhardt never lost a step. He just kept going.

To win, a driver has to have courage, has to have

*Dale Earnhardt takes the checkered flag in winning effort at
Daytona International Speedway.*

guts. Dale Earnhardt's gutsiness is one reason that he has won some 70 races. In all of stock car racing history, only a small handful of drivers have won as many.

Every time a car enters a turn, courage is a factor. "The race is won or lost on the corners," says one

Jeff Gordon, winner of ten races in 1996, is often hailed for his abundance of natural talent.

crew member. "It's easy to fly down the straights. You just put the gas pedal on the floor. But you can't do that on the corners. You'll shoot into the wall.

"The difference between winning and losing is how much you slow down on the corners, how often you lift your foot from the gas pedal or go for the brake." Since the race can be decided by a part of a second, just one lift of the foot more than one's closest rival can be costly.

Ernie Irvan is another driver who is known for being aggressive. In 1994, Irvan hit the wall at the Michigan International Speedway and suffered life-threatening injuries. But after a year on the sidelines, Irvan was able to return to racing. He won twice in 1996.

Irvan, in fact, has been criticized for driving too aggressively. It's been said that his hard driving has caused accidents. Irvan defends himself, blaming it on the speed at which cars travel. "When you're taking a football field a second," he says, "people don't realize what kind of things we're going through in the car."

Other drivers, while being aggressive, put more stress on their ability, on their natural talent for the sport. Jeff Gordon, Terry Labonte, Bill Elliott, and Rusty Wallace are in this category.

Drafting—driving close behind another car—enables the trailing car to travel faster while using less fuel.

Whether a driver relies more on his natural ability or his or her boldness, winning also involves being sharp and quick to react. You have to know how to meet the challenges as they occur.

When race speeds mount toward 150 miles an hour and beyond, *pushing* can be a problem. A driver has to be able to recognize the condition and respond correctly.

"Pushing" has nothing to do with nudging the car in front or being shoved from behind. When a car is pushing, it "tries" to go straight when the driver wants to turn. The wall suddenly looms up. A shattering head-on crash can be the result.

When pushing occurs, the driver can't attempt to muscle the car around the turn. That can increase the car's tendency to push. It takes a gentle touch to get the car to do what you want it to do. To correct the problem, a crew member adjusts the setting of jackscrews on the car's rear wheels during a pit stop. Adding air pressure to the left rear tire can also help.

Looseness is another serious problem. Also called oversteering, looseness occurs during a turn. It's when a car's rear end suddenly loses its grip and swings toward the front end. Looseness can be caused by too much weight at the car's rear or springs that are too stiff. The problem can usually be corrected during a pit stop.

Every stock car race has its strategic aspects. Race strategy commonly involves *drafting,* the art of driving inches behind another car at high speed. Drafting enables the driver of the following car to take advantage of the reduced air resistance behind the lead car.

If the driver in the trailing car can keep within that low pressure zone, his car will move faster while using less fuel. It's something like being towed. Sometimes a line of several cars will run nose-to-tail, each being pulled along by the car in front.

Darrell Waltrip once won the Daytona 500 by stretching his gas mileage by drafting. As the race came down to the final laps, Waltrip's crew chief figured out that Ken Schrader, the race leader, was going to have to make one more pit stop for fuel. But if Waltrip, who was running second, could avoid making a stop, he could move past Schrader and win.

"We're going close on gas," his crew chief radioed Waltrip. "Be conservative. You need to draft everybody."

Waltrip began to draft every car he could find. He

Yellow caution flag at Daytona International Speedway after Ed Howell hit the wall and was then smacked by second car driven by Will Hobgood. Neither driver was seriously hurt.

was drafting when Schrader made his pit stop. As Schrader took on fuel, Waltrip surged into the lead.

On the next to last lap, Waltrip gasped when he saw a red warning light on his dashboard go on, a signal that he was running out of fuel. He reported the flashing light to his crew chief. "Don't get excited," the crew chief said. "Shake the car around. Keep shaking it." The crew chief knew that there were still tiny pockets of fuel inside the fuel cell. Shaking the car, swerving from left to right, and back, would release the fuel. The strategy worked, and when Waltrip crossed the finish line and took the checkered flag, his fuel tank was bone dry.

Sometimes, of course, race conditions can frustrate a driver's strategy. A mishap during a race can cause the yellow flag to be waved. It's a signal to drivers to slow down and drive in single file, each driver holding to his position. Once the problem is corrected, drivers resume racing speeds.

As all of this suggests, it's not easy to win in Winston Cup competition. In fact, for most drivers, winning doesn't happen very often, if at all. Look at what happened in 1996. There were 31 races that season, but only eleven drivers got to visit victory lane. Jeff Gordon, with ten victories, headed the list. Rusty Wallace was a winner five times; Dale Jarrett, four times. Fifty-six drivers never won even once. Obviously, being a winner demands special qualities.

broadsided—During a race, for a disabled car to be hit on the driver's side by another car; also called getting "T-boned."

caution flag—The yellow flag used to warn drivers of danger on the course.

chassis—A car's frame and wheels on which the body is supported.

checkered flag—A flag patterned with white and black squares that signals a driver that he is winner of the race.

downforce—Heavy downward pressure created by airflow and drag.

drafting—To follow close behind another car at high speed to take advantage of the reduced air resistance.

drag—Anything that works to retard the car's forward motion.

engine block—The heavy casting that contains the cylinders and other of the engine's moving parts.

green flag—The flag that signals the start of a race and that the course is clear.

groove—The shorter, fastest, and safest route around a track.

hauler—The huge tractor trailer that transports race cars, along with spare parts, equipment, and supplies; also called a transporter.

kart—A miniature automobile with a tubular chassis used for racing.

lap—One complete circuit of the race track.

looseness—At high speed, when a car's rear tires lose their grip on a turn and the rear end begins to swing toward the front end as a result.

NASCAR—National Association of Stock Car Auto Racing, the governing body of stock car racing.

pace car—The car that leads the field of competitors through the pace lap and parade lap.

pace lap—Led by the pace car, a complete circuit of the race course taken by the field to permit the engines to warm up and allow the cars to approach the starting line at top speed.

parade lap—Led by the pace car, a complete circuit of the race course taken by the field to give spectators a view of the cars before the race begins.

pit—The area just off the track where cars are refueled, repaired, and tires are changed during a race.

pole position—In a race, the starting position in the front row closest to the infield.

pushing—At high speed, the tendency of a car to plow straight forward in a turn.

set up—To prepare a car for a race through the adjustment of various components, such as shock absorbers, springs, etc.

spoiler—The long, narrow metal plate mounted on the car's rear deck that breaks up the flow of air and creates traction.

tachometer—A dashboard instrument that reports the revolutions per minute of the car's engine.

transporter—The huge tractor trailer that carries race cars from one track to the next, along with spare parts and supplies; also called a hauler.